AUSTRIA

A PICTURE MEMORY

Text
Bill Harris

Captions
Nicola Dent

Design
Teddy Hartshorn

Photography
Colour Library Books Ltd.
The Austrian Tourist Board

Editorial
David Gibbon

Production
Ruth Arthur
Sally Connolly
Neil Randles

Director of Production
Gerald Hughes

CLB 2928

This 1993 edition published by Magna Books,
Magna Road, Wigston, Leicester LE18 4ZH
Printed and bound in Singapore
ISBN 1-85422-580-4

AUSTRIA

A PICTURE MEMORY

MAGNA BOOKS

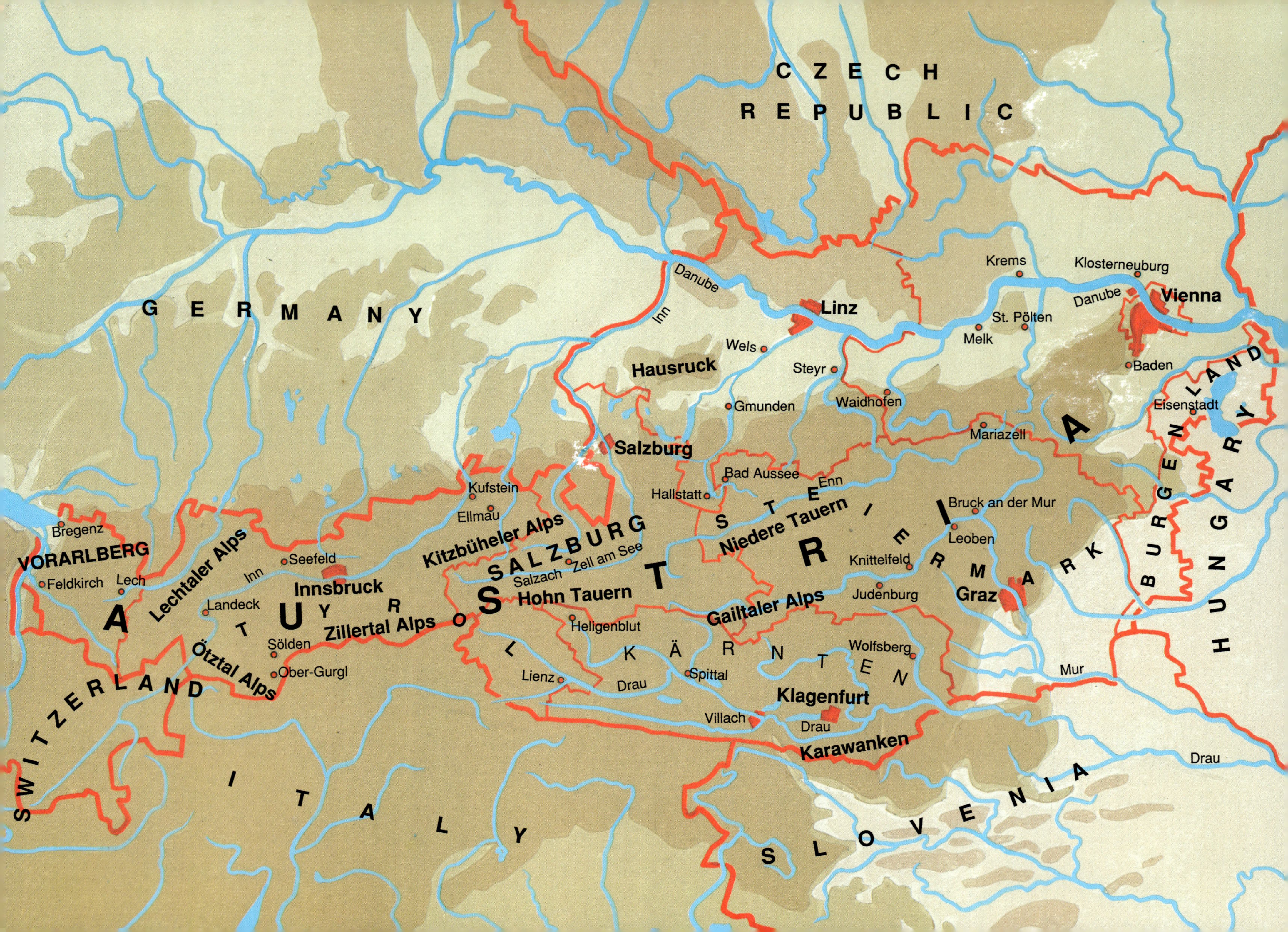
CZECH REPUBLIC
GERMANY
AUSTRIA
HUNGARY
SLOVENIA
ITALY
SWITZERLAND
VORARLBERG
TYROL
SALZBURG
STEIERMARK
KÄRNTEN
BURGENLAND
Vienna
Klosterneuburg
Krems
Danube
St. Pölten
Melk
Baden
Eisenstadt
Linz
Wels
Steyr
Hausruck
Gmunden
Waidhofen
Mariazell
Salzburg
Bad Aussee
Hallstatt
Enn
Niedere Tauern
Bruck an der Mur
Leoben
Knittelfeld
Judenburg
Graz
Kufstein
Ellmau
Kitzbüheler Alps
Zell am See
Salzach
Hohn Tauern
Gailtaler Alps
Heligenblut
Wolfsberg
Mur
Spittal
Lienz
Drau
Klagenfurt
Villach
Karawanken
Bregenz
Feldkirch
Lech
Lechtaler Alps
Inn
Seefeld
Innsbruck
Landeck
Zillertal Alps
Sölden
Ober-Gurgl
Ötztal Alps

First page: the Austrian state flag, which differs from the national flag in that it features a black eagle and coat of arms in the center. In addition, each of Austria's nine provinces has its own separate flag and arms. Previous page: the charming Tyrolean village of Ellmau, backed by the Kaiser Mountains.

The great Austrian Empire existed for nearly a century longer than the Roman Empire, but the glories of its history are not usually remembered with images of clattering armies and triumphal marches. In Austria, military might wasn't usually the center of attention because the people were far too busy creating music and poetry, feasting and dancing, enjoying their beautiful countryside and enhancing it with buildings designed as a feast for the eyes. It wasn't that they didn't have a high regard for their soldiers, but it was uniforms, decorations and dashing manners that impressed them most, and what an officer did on the battlefield was not nearly as important as the figure he cut on the dance floor.

In the history of the world, most empires have been built by kings pushing beyond their borders and fighting with anyone who tried to stop them. But when Count Rudolf of Hapsburg began expanding his power in 1272, he founded a dynasty that eventually discovered a better way of adding territory by means of marrying the right people. But using marriage in place of war was not Rudolf's route to greatness. He was a brilliant military man who had conquered most of southern Germany before he became its king and inherited the Holy Roman Empire of Charles the Great. And when he became an emperor king, he was forced to defend his territory against all challengers. Among them was King Premysl Ottokar of Bohemia, who took advantage of the change at the top to solidify his claim to the territory known as Ostmark, the eastern border that marked the boundary between Christendom and Byzantium. When Rudolf accepted the challenge and killed Ottokar on the Plain of Marchfield, across the Danube from Vienna, he moved into the city and made it the center of his empire, and it remained so until 1919.

But its early days were grim for the Austrians, who considered the German Hapsburgs foreign intruders. And, for more than a century, fighting over who was entitled to follow Rudolf as emperor kept the country on edge. The situation hit its lowest ebb in the mid-15th century as two brothers were battling furiously for control, in a fight that seemed destined to leave the victor with a ruined land, but then fate took a hand. One of the brothers died suddenly, and in 1463 the survivor, Friedrich of Styria, was crowned king of Germany and named emperor by the Pope, a move that gave him the right to pass his titles and his lands to his descendants. His son, Maximilian I, expanded the Hapsburg holdings into the low countries and Burgundy, by marrying the daughter of King Charles the Bold, and although he was eventually called upon to defend what he had gained, he added even more territory to the empire by winning the fight. Maximilian's son followed in his father's footsteps, taking control of Spain and its American colonies as well as kingdoms in Italy, by marrying Mad Joanna, the daughter of Spain's Ferdinand and Isabella, and the stage seemed set for a glorious future.

The future was still clouded, though. The Turks were pushing up the Danube in search of slaves and treasure, and in Germany Martin Luther was spreading ideas that would, in another half-century, result in the Austrian-inspired Counter Reformation. This, in turn, led to the disastrous Thirty Years' War that engulfed all of Europe. By the time it was over, and the Turks were finally defeated as well, the Hapsburgs turned their attention to Hungary, and in 1699 gained the hereditary right to its throne as well as territory extending into Transylvania.

When the Hapsburg line in Spain came to an end, France's King Louis XIV decided it was time to contest succession to the Spanish throne and declared war on Austria. The kings of England and Holland, who had no great love for the French, joined the fight, and when it was over the Hapsburgs controlled the southern low countries and the kingdoms of Milan and Naples. It not only enhanced Austria's prestige, but also brought a new cultural influence to Vienna as Belgians and Italians added their cosmopolitan ideas to a mix that until then had been German-dominated. But there was a new crisis brewing. The Emperor Charles VI had no male heir, and the Hapsburg lands were in the same danger of division that had faced the Spanish Empire a generation earlier. Charles solved the problem with a special law allowing his daughter to succeed him and proclaiming the indivisibility of the monarchy. His action also turned the Hapsburg lands from a collection of territories related by marriage into a real empire. Of course, it was a concept that didn't sit well with the nobles in neighboring countries, and when the Emperor's daughter Maria Theresa came to the throne in 1740 she was surrounded by enemies. It took her eight years to establish herself, but once the warring was over Maria Theresa became the mother of her country, and spent the next 40 years working for her people. She inspired unprecedented patriotism among the Austrians and at the same time made the country's multi-national population eager to work together, something that had never happened before. But Austria had never had an empress before and never would again. In 1793 Maria Theresa's daughter, Marie Antoinette, was executed in the French Revolution, and the history of Europe took yet another turn against the old style.

Still, the House of Hapsburg held on, even though absolute monarchies had obviously become outdated. The Austrians were so appalled by the death of their princess that Vienna became a center of anti-revolutionary thought, and by the beginning of the 19th century Austria stood alone with Russia and the newly-emerging Prussia as the only such monarchies left in the world. It survived uprisings at home and revolutions in its Italian and Hungarian territories. It survived a war with Denmark and another with Prussia. And the Austrian people survived a succession of emperors both good and bad. When the revolution finally came, it was one that could only have happened in Austria.

It began in the midst of the *Fasching*, the pre-Lenten carnival that was in that year, 1848, one of the most dazzling ever seen in Vienna. The balls were spectacular, Franz Liszt was performing to sold-out houses and Jenny Lind was stealing everyone's heart with her sweet voice. But outside in the streets, students were demonstrating to "liberate our emperor from his enemies." Their picketing went virtually unnoticed until three weeks later when they gathered to decide what to do next, and they were inspired by a speech calling for such reforms as a free press, trial by jury and a representative assembly. When the speech ended, the demonstrators turned into a mob. Violence broke out, people were shot, and the rampage lasted for two days, until the emperor himself appeared in an open carriage, promising them "You shall have everything, everything!"

But by then it seemed as though everything might already be lost. In the next few days there were anti-government demonstrations in Milan, in Budapest, in Prague. The emperor knew he was in trouble, and during the next few months it began to look very much as if he would be the last of the Hapsburgs. But there was a strong woman waiting in the wings in the person of Archduchess Sophie of Bavaria, who had become obsessed with the idea of holding the family together, for which she had very good reason.

Emperor Ferdinand soon moved from Vienna to Innsbruck, and from there watched Hungary secede from his empire. He watched as Venice reestablished itself as an independent republic and helped the Czechs establish their own government. Meanwhile, Archduchess Sophie bided her time. She had decided long before that she would one day be Empress of Austria, or at least the mother of an emperor, and opted for the latter when her son Franz Josef was born. The events of 1848 gave her the opportunity she was waiting for. The boy's father was the heir apparent, but Sophie considered that a minor detail, and while all of Austria wondered whether the empire might be sliding off into history, she went to work. But all her work was behind the scenes, because when the inevitable crisis came she wanted her son to appear as the savior of his country. Her scheming worked. When Ferdinand announced that the time had come to put the empire in the hands of a younger man, it came as quite a surprise that the man he had in mind was his nephew. Franz Josef was 18 years old at the time. He would be Emperor for the next 68 years, and his mother would be at his side for 25 of them.

Franz Josef was a strong leader, but his reign was dogged by personal tragedy. His brother, Maximilian, the self-styled ruler of Mexico, was gunned down by a firing squad halfway around the world; his wife, whom he loved but neglected, was stabbed to death by an assassin, and his son, the crown prince, committed suicide. Finally his nephew, Franz Ferdinand, the new heir to the throne, was assassinated at Sarajevo in 1914, and two weeks later Franz Josef signed the order that began the First World War. Two years later the Emperor was dead, and before much longer the Austrian Empire ceased to exist.

The new Emperor, Karl, signed away his right to rule and Austria became a republic after November 11, 1918. Karl also signed treaties that made Hungary and Czechoslovakia independent, granted territory to

Romania and Poland, and gave Serbia the lands that eventually became Yugoslavia. In Austria itself, the First Republic was a disaster, and in 1938 it fell to the German National Socialists and was incorporated into Hitler's Reich. When the war ended, the country that was once the heart of a great empire was divided into four zones, controlled by the British, the French, the Soviets and the Americans. The occupation ended 20 years later, on October 26, 1965, when the four powers recognized Austria as a sovereign independent state with its own constitution and a democratic government.

The country that emerged is quite different from the one that existed in the glory days of the Hapsburgs. It was reduced to what was left over after the demands of its neighbors had been satisfied, and the demands included its access to the sea, as well as huge chunks of land that were part of the original country before it was expanded into an empire. The resulting territory averages about 350 miles from west to east and 175 miles from north to south. Its 32,000 square miles are contained within an unusually long frontier that stretches 1,650 miles and forms borders with seven different countries. Austria's ethnic character was altered, too. Over its history, the empire had been a polyglot of different cultures, but now it is 98 percent Germanic. On the other hand, if the Germans and the Austrians are kissing cousins, the romance in their souls is quite different.

Although it is foolish to make generalizations about any culture, there is an undeniable joy in the Austrian outlook that is more restrained among the Germans. Music has been close to Austria's heart since before the Romans arrived, and the average Austrian can be as enthusiastic about a hand-cranked barrel organ as about a grand opera. The Golden Age of music in Vienna arrived in 1762, when Christoph Gluck broke new operatic ground with his *Orfeo* at a time when Josef Haydn was developing the form that every symphony now follows, as well as the pattern for string quartettes and sonatas. As the conductor of the court orchestra of the Esterhazy princes, Haydn's was a name to be reckoned with when 25-year-old Wolfgang Amadeus Mozart arrived in Vienna from his native Salzburg, and the young man clearly had his work cut out for him. It wasn't easy. First, Mozart antagonized the gentry with his *Marriage of Figaro*, whose central theme was a servant duping his master. Then he got into trouble with *Cosi Fan Tutti*, whose libretto condoned marital infidelity. It didn't matter that Mozart wrote the music and not the words; the Austrians didn't make the distinction. They finally forgave him when he gave them *The Magic Flute*, but although the opera turned his luck, the composer was down on his fortune for most of his short life. Not a note of his music ever showed it, though, and today Mozart is widely regarded as the greatest composer Austria, or any other country, has ever produced. But he is far from the only one.

Ludwig van Beethoven arrived in Vienna from Bonn in 1792, the year after Mozart died, and his obvious talent as a pianist made him an instant favorite among the Viennese. His new neighbors also recognized his genius as a composer, but Beethoven himself was not enthusiastic about them, and although he obviously loved the city, he never courted its citizens. In spite of it, they lionized him at the same time as they were studiously ignoring one of their own. Franz Schubert, a former member of the court's boys choir, wrote his first symphony at the age of 17, and in the next 14 years set more than 600 German romantic poems to music, creating a new form of *Lieder*. During the same period he turned out beautiful masses, great symphonies and other works, but before he died, at the age of 31, only one concert of his work was ever given in his native city.

Most of the great composers who spent their finest hours in Vienna are so much a part of the whole world today that, except to the most sophisticated listeners, their music doesn't always conjure up images of the city on the Danube. But the very name Strauss, even before the first note is heard, instantly says Vienna to everyone. Johann Strauss was born there in 1804, and when he was 15 years old he formed a musical group with other youngsters in much the same way as today's teenagers form rock groups. Before long they were so much in demand that they split into two orchestras, one headed by Strauss and the other by the equally famous Joseph Lanner. Though close friends, they entered into a spirited competition for the title of Waltz King, an honor that went to Strauss after he added a new style to the musical form that made Vienna famous. Lanner represented the romantic traditions of the city, but Strauss added the fire of the Gypsies to bring a kind of frenzy to his music, and his listeners adored him for it. When the King died, the mantle fell to his son, Johann Strauss the Younger. Many feel he outdid his famous father and by the time he was in his mid-20s he had more than 300 musicians working for him, and personally appeared to conduct a half-dozen orchestras each night. He still had time left over to write more than 160 waltzes, each quite different from the others. The best known of these, *The Blue Danube,* is the unofficial national anthem of Austria – high praise considering that the official one was written by Mozart.

When the waltz first appeared on the banks of the Danube in the 1770s it was considered scandalous in some circles because the dancers actually touched one another, and dangerous in others because of the speed required to keep up with the music. It was banned in many places, but the Viennese, who had always loved dancing in any form, took to it instantly. Their enthusiasm was contagious, and before too many years went by the minuet ceased to exist in the capitals of Europe.

The new dance required new settings, and the inventive Austrians were quick to provide them in the form of huge dance halls with plenty of room for the sweeping, revolving steps the waltz demands. They were the precursors of today's discos, lavishly decorated with mirrors and crystal chandeliers and with floors so highly polished to make the gliding steps easier that they were more like ice-skating rinks than dance floors! The largest of them could accommodate 5,000 dancers, and it was filled to capacity every night. Its circular ballroom was surrounded by mirrors reaching up to a ceiling elaborately painted with scenes from Greek mythology. Niches around the room were faced with colored glass illuminated from behind, and beyond were other rooms where dancers could retire to catch their breath, including a dozen intimate dining rooms and a grotto where after-dinner coffee was served in a setting that reminded everyone of their beloved Vienna Woods. But it was only one of dozens of similar dance halls. At the same time, there were balls every night: at the court of the Emperor, at embassies, at military quarters and even in the homes of the middle class. The fancy-dress balls, quite possibly the most glittering affairs ever seen, all followed the same basic form. They began with a sumptuous buffet and, when the music began, the preliminaries included a Polonaise, most often by Chopin, followed by a quadrille, all calculated to build toward the waltz itself, somewhat like athletes warming up! Then, when the orchestra began playing the latest Strauss creation, everyone was on their feet and the beautiful, fast movement usually didn't stop until sunrise.

Johann Strauss the Younger often said that his music pleased his fellow Viennese not because it represented something good that was happening in their midst, but because it made them happy "in spite of everything." But he caught their national spirit in the leitmotif of his great operetta *Die Fledermaus,* which tells us: "Happy is he who forgets what cannot be changed."

Facing page: the Bergkirche at Eisenstadt, the capital of Burgenland. Within this fine building the body of the city's great composer Josef Haydn was re-interred in 1820.

Vienna (these pages) boasts a wealth of attractive and elegant buildings in a range of architectural styles. These include the Renaissance-style Burgtheater (bottom left) and State Opera House (left), and the Greek Revival-style Parliament building (top left). This beautiful city is also home to the palaces of Schönbrunn (above and facing page top) and Belvedere (below and facing page bottom), both set amid lovely gardens and considered to be among Europe's finest.

JOHANNES BRAHMS

Vienna is internationally renowned for the part it has played in the history of classical music. Birthplace of Franz Schubert and Johann Strauss, this musical city was also home to Beethoven, Haydn, Brahms and many other fine composers. Tributes to these famous men include the memorial to Strauss the Younger (below), the monument to Brahms (facing page bottom), and the preserved house and contents of Pasqualatihaus (facing page top), where Beethoven once lived.

Facing page: Vienna offers a whole host of attractions that range from the Giant Wheel (top) in Prater Park to boat trips along the Danube Canal (bottom). St. Stephen's Cathedral (above), street cafés on fashionable Kärntnerstrasse (top right), and the Museum of Fine Arts (bottom right) on Maria-Theresien-Platz, also draw visitors. Equally popular are the exhibits at the Wagenburg Coach Museum (right) and dressage displays at the Spanish Riding School (below).

A magical, snow-dusted view o ephansdom and its surroundings (below) clearly illustrates th na is as beautiful by night as it is by day. The distinctive p t. Stephen's Cathedral and the floodlit dome of the grand K e dominate the skyline. Facing page: ornate lampposts lend a ming glow to the Rathausplatz and contrast with the soaring spires of the city's magnificent cathedral, a prominant landmark in Vienna.

Lower Austria (these pages), the country's largest province, is an area of great charm characterized by rolling valleys and picturesque settlements. Its main town, Krems (below), is not only the oldest and most historic place in the state, but is also a thriving center for the wine industry. Facing page: two other delightful towns in the province are Klosterneuburg (top), dominated by the twin spires of its Augustinian Abbey, and picturesque Waidhofen (bottom), located on the River Ybbs.

With the mighty Danube and its tributaries, sunny slopes (bottom left), and rich soil, Lower Austria (these pages) has proved to have ideal conditions for the cultivation of vines (below). Wine tastings and traditional festivals (center left) are a frequent occurrence, especially in the Danube Valley's delightful Wachua region, between Krems and Melk. Left: Weissenkirchen, seen beyond the vines, is one of many pretty market towns scattered throughout Wachua.

Baroque architecture at its most splendid is to be seen in Lower Austria's Benedictine abbeys at Melk (top left and facing page bottom) and Altenburg (facing page top), contrasting with the more restrained exterior of the schloss (left) at Niederweiden, and the colorful houses in historic Krem (above). Bottom left: vine-covered slopes at Spitz, and (below) a vineyard in ancient Retz – signs of the area's flourishing wine trade.

APOTHEKE

Conveniently located between Vienna and Salzburg is the impressive city of Linz (below), third-largest in the country and capital of Upper Austria. Overlapping this beautiful province is the stunning Salzkammergut or "Lake District," renowned for its numerous lakes and its idyllic, lakeshore towns, nestling at the foot of mountains. Among these are St. Wolfgang (left), Gmunden, with its picturesque Schloss Ort (bottom left), and Hallstätt (overleaf). Center left: the Danube loop.

The province of Styria (these pages) has plenty to offer both residents and visitors alike. Known for the excellent walking (below) this mountainous region affords, Styria has also received international acclaim for the white horses (left) bred at the Lippizaner Stud at Piber. Among the state's many scenic towns are Mariazell (top left), Bad Aussee (above) and Oberwölz (facing page top), and the larger city of Graz (bottom left and facing page bottom).

At the southern end of Styria's narrow Mur valley is Graz, Austria's second-largest city and capital of the province. A fine university town and industrial center, the city boasts a number of impressive structures that include the grand Town Hall (facing page bottom), with its splendidly ornate interior (facing page top). North of Graz is Rein, with the lavishly decorated Cistercian Abbey (below) as its chief attraction.

SORAVIA

The attractive city of Salzburg (below), capital of the province of the same name, has grown up along the banks of the Salzach River at the foot of three wooded hills. In addition to its superb surroundings the city boasts the lovely, 19th-century Mirabell Gardens (bottom left), with walkways, sculptures, a central fountain and the Schloss Mirabell. Center left: the impressive Hohensalzburg Fortress that overlooks Salzburg, and (left) another fine castle at Anif, to the south.

The spectacular Eastern Alps cover over two-thirds of Austria and attract numerous sport and nature lovers throughout the year. Facing page: the towering peaks of the Bischofsmütze (top), which overlook the village of Filzmoos, and of Mount Wiesbachhorn (bottom), viewed from the Grossglockner High Alpine Road. Below: the formidable Tennengebirge range, a daunting challenge that draws many an ambitious climber, and (overleaf) an alpine band backed by the imposing Hochkönig.

Superb views and perilous hairpin bends combine to make traveling the Grossglockner High Alpine Road (these pages) a truly memorable experience. One of the most beautiful mountain highways in the world, it stretches some 50 miles from Zell am See to Heiligenblut (overleaf), a mountaineering center overlooked by Austria's highest peak, the mighty Grossglockner. Center left: Franz-Josefs-Höhe, one of the highway's excellent lookouts, commands stunning views of the mountains.

CAFE RESTAURANT

Located at the heart of the Alps, and a wonderland of snowy peaks and forest-clad slopes, the beautiful Tyrol (these pages) is a province that captivates many. Jochberg (bottom left), Going (above), Kufstein (facing page bottom) and Ellmau (overleaf) are all superbly situated along the lovely Inn Valley, which stretches for some 100 miles through the region. Popular Tyrolean pastimes include skiing, at scenic resorts like Upper Zillertal (left), climbing, hiking, and traditional sleigh rides (below).

A different side of the Tyrol is revealed during the summer months, when rolling green meadows, prolific harvests, and a profusion of vivid blooms replace the white blanket of winter. The fertility of these Alpine valleys is clearly evident around Wiesen (facing page top and below), in the Kaunertal region (facing page bottom), and at Zirl (overleaf), whose verdant slopes contrast with the Nordkette range beyond.

The Tyrolean capital, Innsbruck (below) is located on the right bank of the River Inn, beneath the formidable crags of the Nordkette. Among its elegant throughfares are Maria-Theresien-Strasse (right), the city's main shopping area, which leads to the old town. Full of character and color, this part of the city is known for its fine Hofburg Palace (bottom right) and for its traffic-free Herzog-Friedrich-Strasse (center right), with the famed Little Golden Roof at its north end.

TAXI

Austria Tabak

Twice host to the Winter Olympics, and an excellent year-round resort, Seefeld (facing page bottom) offers a wealth of attractions. One of these is its remarkable outdoor swimming pool (facing page top), dramatically overlooked by snowy peaks that include the formidable Karwendel range (right and below). Close by is the superbly sited village of Mösern (above), and to the southwest the ski resort of Igls (bottom right). Top right: the splendid Mutters and Natters mountains.

Facing page: the Austrian Tyrol is famed for the idyllic charm of its beautiful villages and the grandeur of mountains such as Massereith (top) and formidable Biberkopf (bottom). Below: Imst, a thriving market town dominated by the distinctive village church and its soaring steeple. Overleaf: the Cistercian Abbey of Stams, in the Upper Inn Valley, was founded in the 13th century, rebuilt in the Baroque style in the 17th, and restored in the 1960s.

The Ötztal Valley (the
Valley, following the c
its length lie several popu
one of the highest being the
(below). A little lower down ar
and its sister ski resort Sölden (le

HOTEL KRONE

Breathtaking walks (facing page top), an ornately painted house (above), the lovely church in Elbigenalp (below), and a sunset over the Inn Valley (overleaf), all show something of the infinite variety of the Tyrol. Adjoining this state to the west is the Voralberg, also boasting splendid scenery. The "Alpenhorn" is still played (top right) at Lech (facing page bottom and last page), a fine ski center whose road link with neighboring Warth (right) is blocked in winter. Bottom right: Hochtannberg Pass.